NOURISHMENT

A story with a good ending

by Jeannie Sadler

Three seeds were
planted in the soil
to be nourished.

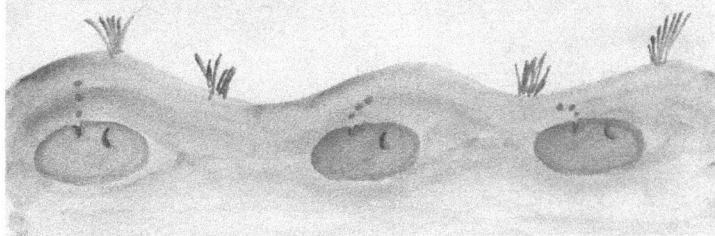

They waited for the sun and the rain.

They each passed the
time in their own way.

One read, one contemplated and one meditated.

But there's no rushing
the sun and the rain.

One day a cloud
ran across the
sky dropping rain
along the way.

There was just enough
for two of the seeds.

The sun chased
the cloud away
and cast it's rays.
The same two
seeds caught the
rays and held
them close.

They were
nourished. They
began to grow.

The other seed sat
alone. It read,
contemplated and
meditated. It
waited for the sun.
But the sun never
came.
Nor did the rain.

One day the seed
decided to break
through the soil.

The soil was dry.
There were pebbles
and rocks.
Breaking through
the soil was hard...
Especially without
nourishment.

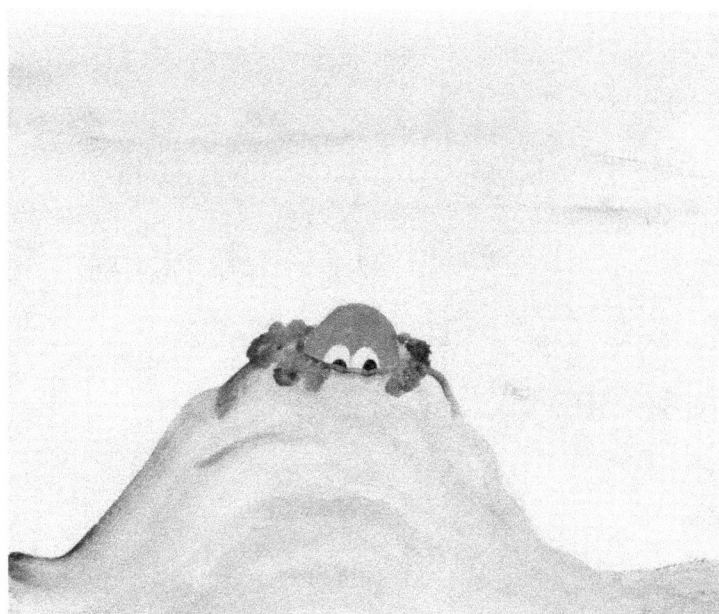

When the seed looked up at the sky, it was cloudy.

One drop of rain
fell and the seed
scrambled to catch
it.

It sprouted.

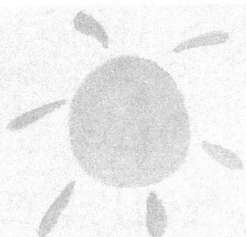

One leaf and one flower.

It grew roots.
With a flying
leap it landed...

And burrowed

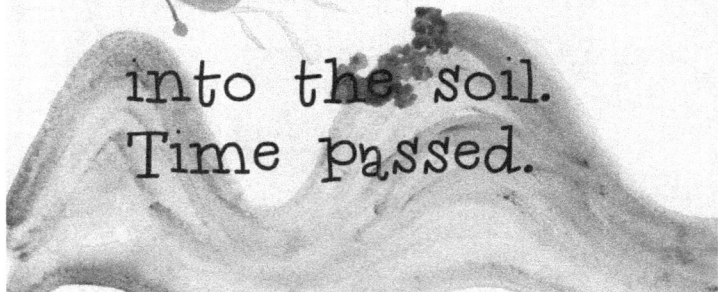

into the soil.
Time passed.

It reached for the sun and the rain. It grew and was beautiful.

The seed knew 2
things;
If nourishment is
slow in coming, or
doesnt come at all,
blooming may be
hard but...
NOT IMPOSSIBLE.

AND

It's okay to be original.

BLESSINGS

the end

onemightybigwish
.com
A purveyor of tall
tales and wondrous
treasures